South African
VERSES

© **Sakura Book Publishing 2025**

Colorful cultures flowing side by side,
In our garden of unity, where hope and kindness greets these pages.

Email: alta@sakurabookpublishing.com
Sakura Book Publishing, Durban, South Africa
www.sakurabookpublishing.com

South African Verses
ISBN: 978-1-0370-2979-0(print)

978-1-0370-2980-6(e-book)

This project is proudly brought to you by Charles and Alta Haffner
- SAKURA BOOK PUBLISHING

All rights reserved. No part of this publication may be reproduced, distributed, or transmitted in any form or any means, including photocopying, recordings, or other electronic or mechanical methods without the prior written permission of the author and publisher, except in the case of brief quotations embodied in critical reviews and certain noncommercial uses permitted by copyright law.

Foreword
Charles R. Haffner

Intern (Editing and Curating)
Ekta Somera

Authors

Alta H. Haffner
James N. McManus
Brett "Fish" Anderson
Vijayan Vengadachellam
Sonia Naidoo
Richard J. Mann
Vishnu Kristna
Ekta Somera
Kivash Hariram
Gavin Prinsloo
Verosha Sewpaul-Naicken
Cassandra Johst-Saayman
Stuthukile Mkhize
Mervin M. Francis
Sarita Mathur
Sinobom Vutha
Bianca Nikita
MaShezee
Zubair Bobat
Timia Chetty
Willhelm

South African **VERSES**

About this Book

South African verses is a collaboration of twenty-two writers from South Africa and one International writer that has books available in South African libraries and bookstores. In these verses, you will find love, happiness, anger, fear and acceptance. From the pens of the young and old, we bring you South African Verses.

South African **VERSES**

Foreword

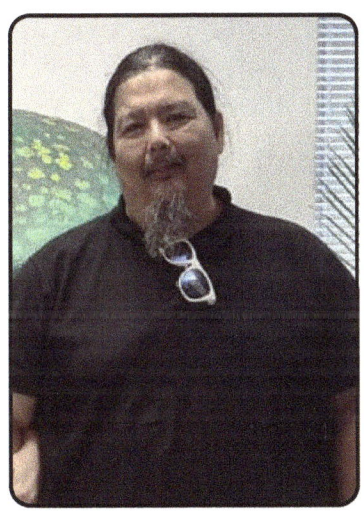

The Republic of South Africa is a land that I now know. From the mountains, desert, ocean, and grassy plains are images that I dreamed of instead of studying. A home of many cultures and ideas that match its beauty. In these pages, you will find some love, strength, beauty and humor mixed in with a little pain. Imagine twenty-two different opinions of the same painting! Today we bring you twenty-two writers sharing their words in South African verses.

South African **VERSES**

TikTok: poet Alta H Haffner
sakurabookpublishing.com
alta@sakurabookpublishing.com

Alta H. Haffner is a Haiku poet whose work captures the essence of precious, fleeting moments with simplicity and depth. Born with a deep appreciation for the beauty of brevity, Alta's Haiku poems reflect her keen observation of nature and her ability to evoke emotions in just a few short lines.

Drawing inspiration from the ever-changing seasons, the delicate balance of the natural world, and the quiet whispers of every new dawn, Alta's Haiku poems invite readers to slow down, pause, and appreciate the present moment. With a handful of syllables, she allows her readers to contemplate.

Her passion will always be to inspire other writers to get their books published to an international audience. "I believe all writers should have a book with their name on it" ~ Alta H Haffner

SAKURA BOOK PUBLISHING - sakurabookpublishing.com
Directors: Charles R Haffner & Alta H Haffner (South Africa)
James N McManus - (USA Partner)
Ekta Somera - Publishing Intern

A South African Tanka

a golden red sun
soft azure clouds of heaven
a black night resting

first leaf opening slowly
doves soar in peacefulness

Till my last breath

Hold my hand
Our fingers grasping onto a final
lasting memory,
walking on the warm golden sand
beneath our African sky at dusk

Dedicated to PINK PITBULL - Joleen

Through your Seasons

Let your voice be heard,
you are enough,
even in your downpour of emotions
drenched with tearful memories
of your past.

You are enough.
Through all your seasons,
you will rise,
in your strength.

— Alta H. Haffner

South African **VERSES**

Instagram @j.n.mcmanus
TikTok @j.n.mcmanus

James, a renowned poet and author, has traversed the world's most austere landscapes, now residing in a serene New England coastal village.

His writing embodies a raw, unbridled spirit, distilling life's experiences into poignant poetry. By pairing thought-provoking art with verse, James offers a glimpse into his soul, showcasing his unique genius.

As an accomplished author, James has garnered global acclaim for his No. 1 rated contemporary poetry books, "Travels - a Poetic Journey" and "Poetry From Afar."

His diverse style transcends geographical boundaries, earning him contributions to numerous anthologies and publications, including "Our Seasons of Syllables," "Hope is a Group Project," "Feathers for Hena," and most recently, "Hansha - Reflections."

A Poet's Wish

If I could have only one wish in this dwindling time
That has slipped away from this old soul of mine,
It would be to turn back the hands of a clock's time.
If I could have discovered you sooner,
I would have been able to feel your presence just a bit longer
And experience the consequences that your spirit provokes.

If I could have only known on that day,
The day you captured this old poet's words,
Conveyed through an impassioned spirit.
If I could have only known how much I would come to adore you,
To understand how much your presence would replace
This dark void deep inside my soul,
A place that has now become reserved
Only for the diversity of a great nation.

Suppose I could have only understood at that time
How your presence would keep this spirit of mine alive.
I have come to know through time that you
Have always been destined to be part of this story of mine.
For you see, if I had only known,
I would turn back those clock's hands of time,
To tell you that I will forever reserve
A special place in my heart
For the culturally rich, diverse people of the Rainbow Nation.

South African **VERSES**

Instagram: @brettfisha
Podcast link [Out of the Fishbowl]
https://open.spotify.com/show/6u6fq
angmp3AjefLLklry3

Brett "Fish" Anderson is a writer, speaker, and improviser with South Africa's longest running troupe 'Improguise'. Above all, he is an advocate for justice, believing in the power of collective action to co-create a world that works better for everyone. His book, 'i, church' explores the idea that followers of Jesus are meant to be the church, the people of God actively doing the things of God, rather than simply attending church once a week. Brett's core passion is challenging and inspiring people to live out the beliefs they profess. Brett is intentional about expanding his understanding by engaging with voices of people who don't look like him. When not diving into books about justice or race, especially in the context of South Africa, he enjoys exploring fantasy worlds, often through the works of Brandon Sanderson, Patrick Rothfuss, and the newly discovered Nnedi Okorafor. Writing poetry is another of Brett's creative outlets, allowing him to play with words and inspire deeper reflections on life, justice, and human connection. He also owns the world's most famous stuffed dolphin, No_bob, a fitting name because despite being a dolphin, he doesn't bob!

Heritage

it's not okay
to look the other way
and "Let the past be the past"
when the footprints of my father
can still be seen
carved upon the backs
of your mothers

it's not okay
to "Stop bringing up race!"
when the security guard
at Woolworths
is not keeping
pace with me
as i take my time
wandering through the store
making my weekly purchases

it's not okay
to just have a Brown friend
or adopt a Black child
or to know all the lyrics
to Nkosi Sikelel 'iAfrica
before they get quickly
shooed away
by the bellowing out
of the Blou Se Hemel

it's not okay
to be mesmerised
by the colours
of the rainbow

as you drive home
from the airport
oblivious to the
definitive lack of gold
below your gaze
where the rainbow
smashes into the lives
of those scrambling below

it's not okay
to be okay
with the comfortable
when so many others
still live submerged
in the rotting sewage
carved out for them
by the venomous discharges
of your ancestors

it's not okay
to simply be not
when the loud, vibrant
active call
HAS to be anti
as it can never be said
to be found for one
until it is markedly
experienced by all
and until that moment calls
you may not rest

Crowbar

Fathers Matter was the title
of the workshop we had just held
and also etched on the face
of the angry young man
aiming his crowbar at my car window
raining anger against absence
as if each fresh blow
brought an opportunity
to somehow recapture
the present active presence
of a ghost who had never shown up
because of how we all
had collectively failed him

the passenger mirror
smashed and abused
hanging on for dear life
as a reminder to me
that we have to do better
to hold up a reflection
of the humanity that is on offer
even to those who have been
severely overlooked
and dismissed to the trash pile
hidden in the outskirts
where we can choose to ignore them
until a chance encounter
reminds us of the
violence of our betrayal

but a whisper
had gone out that morning
to a small group of men
who had braved the storms
to be present
and active, and positive
against all the odds
their community
was showering them with
and the Hope is
that will grow into a call
and then a shout
and finally a movement
of dedicated men
whose lives will tell a different story

one that will be eagerly passed
from ear to willing ear
that will march through
the spaces in our country
where many fear to tread
and which might even one day
grab hold of
a terrified young man
standing in the dark
crowbar at his feet
and spark in him
the unlikely dream
of the kind of father he might be
to the young boy
watching him from the shadows

Grey's An @ for Me

in a world of ordered black and white
my words tend to escape and take flight
pushing against the norms and traditions
inviting different paths and new expeditions

and so when rules and laws call for us all to obey
i instead paint between the lines in varying shades of grey
interruping reality with possibility
what is with what may be
what we believe with hoped for fantasy

calling others to throw off their shackled chains
and to step into a world that sings to new refrains
one in which we truly embrace
the beauty that is diversity within the human race
where greed gives way to need

Vijayan Vengadachellam

Instagram and Facebook:
Vijayan Vengadachellam.

Vijayan Vengadachellam is a young male poet who is deeply passionate about writing poetry that reflects emotions and personal experiences. He is dedicated to advocating for those who suffer in silence, using his writing as a means to provide a voice for the voiceless. Writing offers Vijayan an escape from the harsh realities of the world, allowing him to enter a dreamlike state that brings peace to his mind and heart, relieving him from the burdens he carries.

One of his proudest achievements is the creation of a deeply meaningful poem titled "And Yet She Was Blamed!", which he considers one of his best works. He hopes that readers will resonate with its message and find a connection to its themes.

A quote that guides Vijayan in life is: *"Don't let your past mishaps blackmail your present to ruin a beautiful future."*

Since you went away

Life goes on, so they say
In all truth, the pain never really went away.
The uncertainty in the change experienced cannot be explained,
The memories of you are all that I have claimed.
Since you went away,
The essence of my soul intermittently dark,
Like a quiet starry night alone in a park.
Your beautiful smile lit up my heart,
Nothing is the same since the day we've been apart.
Your voice as soothing as a newborns laughter,
Your glistening eyes etched in my memory like the vastness of the galaxy.
But most importantly and lastly,
Your aura and love fills my life with never ending happiness, this is no lie,
Unfortunately since you went away,
All I could say was I miss you and this isn't goodbye.

And Yet She Was Blamed!

Her smile faded just as quickly as her heart did,
Running towards peace just as she escaped from hell,
Yet she was blamed.

Judgments clouded her just as darkness prevails over light,
A catalyst to her never-ending torture,
Yet she was blamed.

Harsh words and bruises pinned to her publicly,
While she was pinned down privately yet again...
She was blamed.

Her womanhood taken from her like a thief getting his way,
By force and without humanity,
Yet she was blamed.

A damaged girl she was called while alive,
Yet what a lovely girl she was called after death.

Humanity is exiled nowadays with little hope of return,
A "damaged" person to me is equal to a kaleidoscope,
The more fractures of colours, the more precise the underlying image.

South African **VERSES**

Instagram: @red_sonia_96
@s.k.yphotography
@artist._.sonia
Tiktok: @red_sonia7
Facebook: Sonia Naidoo

Sonia Naidoo is a multi-talented poet, author, ghostwriter, and artist. Born and raised in Durban, South Africa, her passion for literature blossomed at the tender age of four, nurtured by her mother, who taught her to read and write. Sonia's writing journey truly began at the age of fifteen, when she and her best friend started crafting short fanfiction stories inspired by their favorite books. During this time, Sonia also turned to poetry as a way to navigate the challenges of anxiety and depression.

In 2023, Sonia's short story "Nothing but Lights" was featured in the South African anthology 320 Days of Sunshine. The following year, her poem "To All the Vultures" was published in The Paper Trail Literary Journal.

Sonia's debut novella, Traumata: The Seasons of Femininity, delves into profound themes of a young woman's past, identity, resilience, spirituality and transformation.

Three in One

I tread upon a land where histories entwine,
Where ocean winds carry bloodlines afar,
Sea-sand whips at my bare brown legs,
Like the fingertips of my ancestors, calling.
This foreign soil claims my lineage, mine.

The same relentless heat of the sun
Kisses the earth in Gujarat and Egypt.
Skin like turmeric brushed by Durban's street,
Carrying the weight of migrations I may never know.
Do I betray my forefathers by thriving in an alien land?

Indentured ancestors crossed the endless blue,
And searing deserts. Merchants and slaves,
Trading chains for soil, or labour's endless claim.
They toiled beneath the skies of every hue,
Building lives where caste held no fame.

Cairene and Indian blood sings softly in my veins,
A quiet hymn of resilience and pain.
It thrums against the quietest graves

>Of wounds long scarred, yet never quite healed.
>Can one inherit both suffering and strength?
>
>India's shadow lingers in the air,
>Invisible, yet woven through the past,
>Egypt's phantom stitched in every breath,
>Its weight a burden I still feel, though cast.
>What is my place upon this fractured land?
>
>I see the lotus bloom in African streams,
>Its roots submerged in waters not its own.
>Much like myself, divided by these dreams,
>Between the mosque's call and temple bells,
>And in every tale my family tells.
>
>For I am both the salt of ancient seas,
>And sand that holds the scent of Africa's trees.
>A tapestry of colour, frayed but strong,
>A soul that spans three nations,
>Yet, only belongs to one.

LinkedIn and Facebook:
Oliver Tichmann
X: @scufflethe
YouTube: richardjmann

Richard J Mann is a writer specialising in political satire and humour, known for blending sharp wit with insightful commentary. He began his literary journey by writing short stories, unexpectedly winning first prize in a South African Writers' Circle short story competition many years ago, an achievement that marked the beginning of his creative career.

Richard's blog, The Scuffle Continues, has earned significant recognition, ranking among the top 50 satirical blogs on the internet. He has also written for major publications, including Daily Maverick, The Citizen, The Sowetan, and Staffrider, and contributed a story to an SABC radio programme. Despite the challenges faced by freelancers in the industry, his work continues to make an impact. In addition to his online presence, Richard has published five satirical books on Amazon Kindle and has ventured into TikTok and YouTube, where he offers his unique perspective on current affairs.

Currently, Richard is working on his sixth satirical book and co-authoring a collection of short stories titled People of the Valley (working title). Although he remains diffident about poetry, he has made two attempts, which are presented below.

The Circus Comes To Town

I had never been to a circus. That was also true for my classmates and most of the people of Ncalu. I suspect that many of the people in the village of Ixopo had not, either.

Every wheeled vehicle in Ncalu was packed with eager folk on the historic opening night. We travelled the eleven miles to the village in laughing, chattering groups, excitement and anticipation building with each mile travelled. Some of the men fortified themselves with regular sips from bottles in brown paper bags, and they, too, were as merry as the children.

From films and books, we knew of the gaily coloured big top, lions, elephants, spine-chilling and gravity-defying acts. Shivers of delight passed through us as we approached the big tent in an open field.

There were no lions or elephants. A tethered horse grazed disconsolately, and a couple of goats chewed at whatever they could find in the sparse grass. Nothing could dampen our spirits. There was a rush for the ticket office, where a bored, heavily made-up lady chewed gum as if the effort wearied her infinitely.

he ringmaster, bold, breezy and cheesily eloquent, welcomed us. Ah, this was promising to be a memorable night.
"And now," the ringmaster boomed, "Marvel at the death-defying deeds of Ferdinand, the fire-eater. All the way from Brazil, Ferdinaaand!" We clapped and cheered as the muscular Ferdinand, bare to the waist, his body gleaming with oil, bounded into the ring.

It was the first fire-eating act we'd ever seen. Ferdinand blew great gouts of fire in every direction, striking dramatic poses. As I watched him, enthralled, a curious thought entered my mind: I had seen him somewhere before. It was not possible. I had never been to Brazil.

Next came Alonzo the equestrian. His horse-riding tricks were mildly entertaining, but not the stuff of great drama. He bore a strong resemblance to Ferdinand, but was distinguished by a long mop of hair, complete with a piratical ponytail. Never mind, there were plenty of thrills to come.

Boris, the high-wire artist, on a disappointingly low wire, shot glances of what looked remarkably like terror, at the sawdust below. Bald-headed, he too, bore the Ferdinand family resemblance.

A succession of Ferdinand lookalikes went through their less-than-heart-stopping routines. Different hairstyles, beards, moustaches, moles, but the family resemblance was strong.

We realized, before long, that this was no Barnum and Bailey, but we determined to make the best of a rare night out. So we cheered and clapped the Ferdinand lookalikes for far more than they were worth.

The performance was drawing to a close. The indefatigable ringmaster announced 'Mustapha, the Amazing Egyptian Maagiciannnn!' He swaggered on in turbaned splendour and made a low bow. Just then, one of the handymen, dashing across to secure a peg, tripped over a rope. The large hammer landed on Mustapha's slippered foot. The yell of pain and anger was understandably loud:

"Wenzani wena? Msu^&#&@ W$%%^&!"
Mustapha could swear in fluent isiZulu!
The accent was pure Ixopo district.

The rest of the show was worth every penny. Mustapha / Ferdinand / Boris / Alonzo fled into the night, pursued by several men. The ringmaster received a few 'klaps' and kicks in the rear, before he, too, fled into the darkness. Chairs flew into the ring. Parents ushered reluctant children out to safety. The gum-chewing lady, no longer bored, paid, with trembling hands, those who demanded a refund. The horse and goats made their dash for freedom. From a safe distance, we watched the big top collapse in on itself. A fitting finale to a night that had suddenly come alive with drama.

We made the journey back home, well satisfied and with many a tale to tell.

There was, the next morning, not even the slightest trace to tell that the circus had come to town.

No time to die

Dressed in unfashionable black
He sat beside my bed
A clumsy fumble with the scythe
"It's time", he said
I said "Voetsek,
I've debts to pay.
There's mortgages and loans
And debts to love and guilt
Come back another day"
He shook his head and left,
Limping ever so slightly

South African **VERSES**

TikTok: @vish_zn

Vishnu Kristna is a published author specialising in poetry. He holds a Bachelor of Commerce degree from the University of South Africa and also runs his own small business. Stepping Stones is his first published anthology of poetry, which highlights the struggles he faced while growing up and navigating through life. It explores how he overcame these challenges and managed to persevere through adversity to achieve the proud accomplishment of having his first book published.

Vishnu has plans to write more poetry books and to explore other genres, including fiction novels and an autobiography that will reveal the unique aspects of his life, which may surprise many people. In addition to his writing, Vishnu has ventured into acting. In 2024, he starred in his first movie, Broken Promises 5: Vengeance, a proud moment for him as he appeared on the same big screen as the movie stars he once admired. In his spare time, Vishnu enjoys keeping his body fit by going to the gym. He also enjoys reading biographies and listening to podcasts that provide insights into the minds of famous and successful people.

You can find his book online on www.amazon.com. For more information or any questions relating to purchasing the book directly or feedback you can contact the author via e-mail: poeticxpress001@gmail.com

He welcomes and appreciates positive reviews of his written works.

Perseverance

Tears trickle down my long, disillusioned face,
With each excruciating word that travels from my mind to my fiery pen.
The ink on my page is diluted by a torrent river of pain,
That floods my saddened crimson-red eyes,
As memories flow from the deepest, darkest crevices of my soul.
I try to control my emotions that now blur my vision of the words staring back at me on my page,
As the waves of memories in a stormy sea crash against the shores of my mind.

I am perplexed as to not knowing why I am on the waves of this stormy, treacherous journey,
Almost drowning in an ocean filled with pain and anguish that almost completely covers my head.
My heart and soul long for the days when the sun was shining brightly,
And the ocean was so calm with an inviting joyfulness,
That I could spend an entire day swimming in its soothing waters,
As my heart and mind were filled with blissful happiness.
Sadly, gone are those days where the joyous, inviting ocean gave me peace of mind.

It has now aged into a stormy, raging ocean that is anything but inviting,
With sweltering waves that crash forcefully onto my heart and mind,
Causing a crater-sized dent on my perplexed and fragile mind.
As each raging, violent wave came crashing down over me with increasing intensity,
It caught me in a current that almost consumed me and pulled me under.
I struggled with such forceful intensity to escape until my body was too weak to move.

Then I decided to stop struggling and fighting the currents and accepted my fate,
I just kept my body and mind still and closed my eyes, allowing nature to take its course.
Realizing that I was no match for the intensity of this powerful, consuming, raging ocean,
I moved my faith from my own devices and placed it in the greater power of God.

I was completely helpless and put my complete trust in Him, accepting His desire for my life.
At that moment of complete surrender and serenity,
The waves crashed down onto me with increased voracious intensity,
That I was completely submerged and taken deeper into the ocean.
I thought to myself, that was it; I was not going to make it, and my life was over.

I closed my crimson-red eyes and almost passed out as the violent waves engulfed my body.
When I saw the ocean miraculously change from a violent, raging dark body of water,
Into a calm, peaceful liquid covered with a blanket of blinding white light,
I closed my eyes as it penetrated my tired, crimson-red eyes.
After a few seconds, I tried opening my shocked eyes again to witness this unreal spectacle.
Seeing the clouds turn from the darkest grey into the brightest white,
And the sunflower-yellow sun appeared over the clouds, radiantly beautiful,
That it drastically improved my visibility of my surroundings and illuminated my position in the ocean.

As I scanned my location, only then did I realize that I was only a few meters from a tropical island.
I mustered up all the energy I could find and swam to the shore with great enthusiasm.
I reached the shore, and tears of joy rolled down my cheeks onto the sandy beach,
And I was flooded with an exuberance of ecstasy and pleasure from surviving this horrendous ordeal.

I was never more ecstatic to be alive than at that particular moment.
Every breath I took was one of gratefulness and thankfulness to God.
I realized that when all is lost and all avenues are explored and you still can't move forward,
Then surrendering to the higher power of God can do extraordinary miracles in your life,
Helping you in unimaginable ways, and all you need is trust and faith...

Instagram and TikTok:
@ektasomera
https://linktr.ee/ektasomera

Ekta Somera is a South African youth activist, the author of two poetry collections and the founder of Paper Trail Literary Journal. As a community mobiliser, Ekta plays a crucial role in advocating for policy changes to combat youth unemployment in South Africa. Her insightful opinion pieces on social issues and youth concerns have been widely published, and she has been featured as a panelist on prominent media platforms such as ENCA and SABC Morning Live.

Ekta also hosts Lead the Wave, a podcast empowering young people to use their talents to make a difference. Her dedication to youth development and her drive to inspire young South Africans have garnered her significant recognition, including being named among the Mail & Guardian's 200 Young South Africans in 2022. In 2024, she won the Youth Icon category at the Lotus FM Women of Substance Awards. Her work continues to leave a lasting impact on both literature and social activism.

The cost of being young

In the land of freedom and equality,
there are whispers of opportunity,
the young ones remember
distorted promises -
"ah child, you will grow up to be
anything you want to be" -
we grew up
and our dreams were set ablaze
in the labyrinth of a jobless maze.

As hope fades with the longing
for a chance to earn a living,
the young ones realise -
an eagerness to soar becomes
wings jammed on a closed door -
the skills we learn no longer matter,
and our talent goes to waste,
even the brightest minds lose sight
in the shadow of unemployment.

The future of our country
depends on the young ones -
but are we truly free to be
whoever we want to be?

Internal Bleeding

Laughter grits through my ears
but I hear their feelings
it's just a joke -
that's why
it crawls up my spine
and makes me feel funny

I am bandaged with scars
and wounded by reality -
words reach much deeper
than metal through my skin -
they take stabs at heart
and call me sensitive for bleeding

I can't see my face
but they stare with grimace -
my heart prepares
to bare any emotions
as their thoughts swirl
into insults in my presence

Smiles are infectious
but these are wounds -
bleeding from one heart
oozing into another -
as their words stab through
reflecting their insides
like a mirror

Scarred and bruised
by words so cruel
it would only be so easy
to slip into their shoes
and walk down the road
hurting others
the way they do -

But my map
has a different route
and I will not allow
the poisoned bite of their pain
to affect my kindness

Moments in Time

I looked up at the sky today,
and something happened.

A flock of birds,
carrying a string of sound, flew by.
It was the missing chord,
the reason my heart beat off-key.
I felt overwhelmed and excited,
was I having an epiphany?

It was somewhat of an awakening,
a sudden realization
that we travel through clouds
and across the sea
in search of new scenery,
when we can simply look up
at the natural palette of colours
unravelling each day.

And as the birds follow their instinct,
we will find our way.

www.linktr.ee/kivash

Kivash Hariram is an educator, author, poet, and writer. He published his debut book, Precious Poetry, in February 2023, an anthology of poems that marks the beginning of his literary journey. Kivash recently graduated with a B.Ed IP degree, aiming to inspire young people through knowledge and prepare them for the future.

Kivash's passion for poetry began in 2018, although he had written occasional poems long before that. A personal heartbreak sparked his interest in poetry, but it is love that continues to fuel his dedication to the craft.

Looking ahead, Kivash plans to secure a teaching position in Durban while also publishing two books as part of a series titled Sometimes Words Do Come Easy. His aspirations for the year include reading more and exploring other avenues within the world of poetry. Kivash credits The Paper Trail Literary Journal for providing invaluable guidance and support, helping him grow as a poet and author. The journal's commitment to advising both aspiring and established authors has played a significant role in his development.

Love, is it worth it?

I don't think people understand love.
I don't think they realise how worthless
it can actually make you feel,
or the lengths that some people would go for it.
On one side of the spectrum,
we have those that are often referred to nowadays as "simps".
An individual who is a try-hard.
Someone who is head over heels for someone,
and the feeling isn't reciprocated.

Then we get those that don't care.
The people that just thrive off attention.
There's hardly any middle point.
It's usually one side of the spectrum or the other.
So back to what I was saying,
love is one of, if not,
the most complex things known to mankind.

Some people do fine without it,
but then some people can't function without it.
There are, however, different kinds of love.
For instance, a person can love an object
such as their toy, or perhaps they love their pet,
but the real dilemma comes in when they start
to love someone on a possible relationship level.

I mean, you can love your parents, siblings, or family,
hence the reason I didn't say "when they start to love someone else".
To love someone on a relationship level entails not counting.
Not counting the mistakes, arguments, who spent the most money,
who gets jealous or forgives more.
The only thing you should count is, on each other.
This person should never let you down.
You should always be able to count on them, and them, on you.

At some stage in our lives, we have all encountered love.
The good, bad, and ugly.
Yet, somehow, somewhere, and for some reason,
we fixate on the ugly and opt not to stroll back into love's realm,
but believe it or not, we will find ourselves back in it, one day.
Some day.

For an increasing number of people, it's when, not if.
We're humans.
We sometimes crave the presence of another.
It's only natural.
As much as we can try to convince ourselves that love isn't for us,
the heart really does want what it wants.

Neither you nor I can change or control that,
irrespective of whether or not we agree.
There are some things in life nobody can change or control,
and convincing ourselves that love isn't for us,
is one of those things.

TikTok, Facebook, Instagram,
YouTube: *The Soul Whisperer.*

Gavin Prinsloo, residing in Cape Town, South Africa, has been writing poetry for four years. During this time, he has published four books and had his work featured in numerous publications around the world.

In addition to his written work, Gavin now produces narration videos to promote both his own poetry and that of other poets. These videos can be found on TikTok, Facebook, Instagram, and YouTube, where he is known by the pen name *The Soul Whisperer*.

Preparing for War

Stand your ground they said, as my boots were scuffed with dust and dirt and sweat stained the brown overall and web belt, changing the color to a dirty blotchy grey, caked stiff with a crust of expired salt and dried mud.

Be a man they said, as they took my soul and twisted it into every possible shape, breaking down resistance and as each shape did not suit their perception of a blooded warrior, discarded what remained to rebuild with what was left, a mere shell of what was once loved and nurtured by mothers now far, far away.

You are a soldier, they said as the boy was destroyed and only the caricature of manhood remained, bowing and scraping to a mortal god thar was called by everybody's name.

You are ready for battle they said, as the fury of a thousand bullets zipped through the air, slicing away unneeded limbs, and laying bare the agony of observing divine cruelty never before imagined.

You are a hero they said, your blood shed for the remission of the sins of those who called you to arms, your flesh in communion with those whose flesh remained and rotted on forgotten battlefields.

You will never stand alone they said, as the nights called to you to relive the faces and places etched with tracer fire into the depths of mind and soul, to awaken, alone, reliving the shame that follows horror after horror cased in copper jacket and blackened by searing flame.

Salute the flag they say; you stood your ground, you were a man, a soldier, you were ready for this, you proved yourself a hero, you will never stand alone.

What they did not realise is that to prepare for war, a boy does not become a man; war creates a warrior, a being caught and trapped alone between boyhood and manhood, a destination devoid of conscience and human emotion; a place of fear and haunted recollection.

Do we prepare for war, yet again?

To the Young

Ah, my young one,
Your life stretches before you,
Mine flashes before my eyes.
You have so much time,
Yet, everybody dies.

Ah, youth of my dreams,
I had so much time,
Yet, you have barely begun.
You cannot see your future;
Many memories ago, I too was young.

Ah, things of yet to come,
Your eyes sparkle with unfettered hope.
My eyes are dull with memories that could not last.
You walk into a sunlit future,
For me, I walk backwards into a faded past.

Ah, seed of another dawn,
Roots tearing into where you want to be.
My soil is leeched, and the earth is cold.
Your fruits call out to harvest,
I am now barren, for I am old.
Ah, my young one,
Your life stretches before you,
Mine knows a truth sublime.
One day you will be me,
At the end, there is no more time.

Beguilement

She spins her elemental form between heaven and earth,
Her colours in tune with her exuded existence,
Fragrant with scents of life,
Flower petals and leaves cascading in perfumed glory,
Blended with the reek of sodden earth and corruption,
A blend of form and scent,
An alchemy of golden light spilling into the very heart of the void,
Birthing extensions of pulsing life into roving existence.

Her feet planted in the firmament,
Roots reaching for the heart of creation,
Anchoring the subliminal to reality.

Her hands spin the eternal loom of life,
Every breath and form moulded in invisible hands,
The only sign of the magic, the winds howling into the heavens.

Clouds of incandescent colour crown her countenance,
Her natural form not visible to the naked eye,
Swirling clouds laced with streaks of lightning,
As her hair fans across the vaults of the universe,
Thunder voicing her incantations,
Her Voice becoming form.

She is the Mother of creation,
A cycle of life reaching into eternity,
And beyond.
She is Creation's womb.

Verosha Sewpaul-Naicken

Facebook:
Verosha Sewpaul-Naicken

Verosha Sewpaul-Naicken was born and raised in a small town on the KwaZulu-Natal (KZN) coast, in Umkomaas. She faced immense challenges early in life, losing her father at the tender age of 10 and her mother at 20. At 18, she was assaulted by her first boyfriend, an experience that profoundly impacted her. Writing poetry has been her escape and a way to articulate her emotions since she was 10 years old.

Verosha is now a Nuclear Medicine Radiographer by profession and, since 2023, has been happily married to the love of her life. Her story is one of resilience, strength, and the healing power of creative expression.

Silent Torture

The voices, they remind me of what once was,
Happiness, love, and joy are all fleeting memories.
In the bustle of the day, the facade is on,
In the stillness of the night, the darkness seems to grow.
The voices in my head lead me astray,
The voices say, "you will never be worth it," "you will never be okay."
The physical pain, I am used to,
The mental pain, how to deal with it, I have no clue.
Staying home eases the pain, but what do I gain?
I know, things will never be the same.
Exhaustion wrecks my mind day and night,
Letting myself go, that is what I see in sight.
I refuse, I loathe the feeling of emptiness.
Climbing out of the darkness, one hand at a time,
Finding peace and solace will eventually bring me back to life.
Depression and anxiety are their names,
I refuse to live my life in their games.
Conversing with someone I trust, slowly opening my eyes,
Depression and anxiety, I am ready to finally start saying my goodbyes.

Oh, Our Little Ones

Oh, our little ones,
It is finally time to depart.
Oh, our little ones,
Keep our memories closer to your heart.
Oh, our little ones,
There was so much we wanted to say to you both.
Oh, our little ones,
We will forever be watching over you; that is our oath.
Oh, our little ones,
We see your tears and hear your heart's silent prayer.
Oh, our little ones,
We wish we could wrap our arms around you both, layer upon layer.
Oh, our little ones,
We left you both as child orphans.
Oh, our little ones,
Just close your eyes and picture our smiles, long since you've closed our coffins.
Oh, our little ones,
Mom and Dad are so proud of you both, watching from above.
Oh, our little ones,
Your journey henceforth will be of abundant success and never-ending love.

South African **VERSES**

Instagram: @cazluanauthor

Cassandra Johst-Saayman has always been captivated by the concept of love, and writing a romance novel has been a dream she has cherished for as long as she can remember. With the unwavering love and support of her husband, that dream has now become a reality. An ex-lecturer in English and Communication, Cassandra holds an Honours degree in English, and her passion for the power of words runs deep. What's even more impressive is that English is her second language. Known for her sassiness and humour, Cassandra admits she often finds herself in trouble, though her dislike of prison colours has kept her out of the slammer.

She jokes that her superpower is fitting in and making friends, but admits that age may be catching up with her, and she's more interested in avoiding drama than stirring it up. Outside of writing, Cassandra enjoys painting, experimenting with new recipes alongside friends, indulging in cake for breakfast, and belting out off-key karaoke while swinging in her backyard. A professional cocktail taster until the third drink, she's also on a never-ending quest to find the best milkshake in town. Currently travelling the world with her ex-pat husband, Cassandra plans to weave her global experiences into the pages of her next novel.

SHE

She moved. I watch intently as her dark locks of hair playfully dance on the foul stench of decay that invades every moving thing across the land. The people here on the outskirts of Knysna say you get used to it, but somehow, the putrefying smell constantly thrusts itself into your aching nostrils at the most inopportune moment. A moment like this. Unfortunately, the scent is more resilient than my will. Wish it was the only time my will failed. I shake my head slightly from side to side in an attempt to get some relief, unsuccessfully. Sighing, I refocus and set my sights on the most enigmatic phenomenon I could have envisioned. With her slight build, she squares her shoulders.

She is standing in the middle of the match-box jungle in eight-inch stiletto heels, and still, the look on her face leaves no doubt she is exactly where she wants to be. She is slightly built, but that only makes her agile like a panther stalking its prey. She moves with the grace mimicked by the river as it cuts through the earth with dangerous precision. It has been said that the men who hover around her are drawn to her beauty and strength. I, however, can clearly see the ruthlessness with which she executes her whims, and it leaves me with a sense of loss and regret. I find it hard to see anything else except her alluring red lips and how the words that flow from them change the surroundings immediately.

I need to move less but find myself taking in my position in the red dust. The greenery on the edge enveloping me is lush. It would create a sense of abundance and peace in a soundless world. A light breeze is coming in from the east, and it urgently whispers about the possibility of change if I succeed. I wipe the stinging sweat from my brow and snort when I see the dust that sticks to my fingertips. That is the thing about being in a place like this. The dirt almost surrounds you like an invisible suffocating cloud; before you know it, you are covered with the remnants of malice and hate.

I focus my attention on her again. The piece of viciously rare beauty found in this green cage. She is known for wearing red. And the dress is sculpted to her figure like the opening petal of a blood-red hibiscus flower. Every line and pleat flows into the next to create a vision of the unattainable. She turns her head in my direction, and if I didn't know better, I would have said she was looking into my soul. Unfortunately for her, all she would be able to see is the bitter void left behind. I hold my breath until she turns away.

A bead of sweat slowly crawls its crooked way down my brow. This is the first time in my life that a woman has ever made me feel this nervous. I tug at the hard seam of my sleeve and realize that it isn't going to move anywhere. The sleeve is matted down, as is the rest of my outfit. What do you expect in hot, humid weather like this? Or could it be more than the weather that creates this suffocating and dizzying effect on me? I look around at the buzzing insects and the thick green foliage that seem to grow closer and closer by the agonizing second. I have been here for a while and seeing her is a welcome reprieve from the monotony of the day. She never raises her voice. She simply leaned over to the closest man, and he relayed her orders to the rest of us.

We immediately react to his barking, and I find myself running in no specific direction. They are the same orders no matter where we go. Find the children. Subdue the woman. Take out the men. We don't have to shoot them. No. That would be a waste of ammo. Sometimes, she will walk through the roughly built zinc houses, and we will try to put on a show. She likes it when there is a lot of blood before the pathetic excuse of pulverized flesh gives in.

Rumour has it that she was still a little girl when men in uniform came into her home and found her family having dinner. She was only seven when they pried her away from her brother's tiny hands and raped her. Repeatedly. Her mother sat there in silence and prayed to God to protect her son because she didn't have it in her to give her husband another boy. That same husband sat there with lustful eyes, waiting for the second that they were alone to get his hands on her. Again. Some higher-ranking officer walked in to see two of his men with their pants around their ankles and her pinned down between them. He took one look at her father's eager face and instructed some of the other soldiers to drag him outside. They beat him until there was nothing left of the pitiful excuse of a father. Only then did the officer walk over to her. She was still trying to cover herself with her torn dress when he kneeled in front of her and gave her these words.

"There is no excuse for what happened to you today. And for that, I am sorry. Maybe one day, you will find the revenge that you need to be what you were always destined to be. However, I took one of your perpetrators today and made him pay. I hope it will be enough for the time being that I don't leave the evil behind after we depart." He simply stood, gathered his troops, and they vacated the simple settlement that had been born out of need on the edges of the forest. She repeats the words to us before every mission.

Her mother never made her forget that she was the reason they had no breadwinner in the house. They were nearly starving when she walked into the tavern that night, knowing whom she wanted to talk to. At that stage, she was twelve and just starting to attract attention. However, she craved power, and she was there to claim it.

She knew that the settlement was raided frequently because they were looking for the drug operation that was supplying freedom fighters with Mandrax. Not only were they using it to finance their illegal weapons, but they were also given to the runners to make them more complacent in the orders they were given. And after years of living with a burning fire, she found the perfect place to spread her hatred like wildfire.
She was tenacious and quickly grew in the ranks. Today, she is the boss with the power of life and death in her hands. She uses the same techniques she was taught as a child. Beat the evil out of the men. Protect the children and make them crave revenge. And the mothers, you may ask. The mothers are made to beg like her mother failed to do.

I see her hovering at the door of the house I entered. I already dragged the father from his seat and waited for her nod to start. When given, I look down and see the fear etched on his weathered face. He looks so familiar. Or like any one of them. Or do I always see the same face before my eyes when I look down at them? The first hit slides off his cheek. The joints in my fingers absorb the impact. I curl my hand in a tighter fist. It is always hard to land it when they are so sweaty. It is even worse when the tears and snot start. I look up and see her questioning gaze. I feel the calm flood my senses, and I see everything clearly. The blood sprayed from his mouth, hitting the small girl on my left. The wailing of the woman behind me, begging. The weak attempt of the man to lift his hands to protect his face. I hit him in the ribs. I stand over him and stare down. I hit him in the face, his head, and anywhere I could get a hit in. Hit after hit, I see everything in slow motion until he isn't resisting anymore. I wipe the sweat from my brow and feel the warmth of the blood I leave behind. I spit on him. Signing my masterpiece. I wipe my hands on my pants and secure my weapon in my hand before I walk to the door to meet her. Her loving eyes look from my hands to the destruction behind me and then back again.

"Well done. I always knew that you would make me proud someday." I can only nod back, and she lifts my chin to face her. "Come on. We have more work to do, Son."

One Day

I know I am supposed to feel guilty, but I don't. There truly was no other way. I am her mother. It is my responsibility to protect her no matter what it takes. I feel my love for her well up inside, and no words can explain the relief I feel because the deed was taken out of my hands. Truth be told, even though I know what should be done, I would not have been able to let her go if the time came. I have been dreading this moment since this whole war has started. That is the only way I can describe the onslaught against my dignity.

Tears are fleeing my eyes silently because this is what our lives have become. I look down at her face, where I grasp her tightly against my body. She is so perfect. Her nose is slim, and her sullen skin is transparent. With her eyes closed, she looks like she is sleeping. But I know. My body knows. The people who look at me with sorrow in their eyes know. And this is how she will always be, my perfect little girl.

I hear a commotion outside. It still can't drown out the horrible squeak of the rusty fan blade above my head. It was all I had to look at while they were busy. That and the shimmer of dust that lightly fell to the ground, like ash covering the last vestiges of my humanity. I wasn't paying attention before, but now I look around and see the only world my daughter will ever know.

The walls are covered with old egg cartons with various marks and dents. I see the remains of old torn-by-time posters between the spaces left bare. And, of course, the scorch marks that were left behind to teach us the history of hate. That is the only teaching being done in this abandoned school. Once, it was a beacon of hope—a chance to change the past and open the world to children—children who were still innocent in the ways of forced malice and persuaded wrath.

I look at the dusty floor and the blood-stained sheets that barely cover me. A bucket of water from the river can be found in the corner. The young man who helped me was washing his hands carefully, trying to get rid of my sticky blood residue. I have to wonder if it bothers him that he needs to practically scrub his skin raw to be released from our interaction today. Is it worse for him when the baby fights to come into this broken world? At least my girl knew better and knew that anything born from violence is destined to die from it. That is something I prayed she would never have to feel.

There is nothing worse than seeing the look in his eyes and knowing it will hurt less if I stop fighting him. If I surrender to his darkness, somehow, I will find my way back again.

I look at the two young women who helped the man relieve me of my precious burden. Don't misunderstand. I love my girl. There is just no way I could keep her safe on the days that he is particularly vicious. And if he hurts her… that will be my fault.

They are talking and avoiding eye contact with me. I think back to a time when I would have joined them. All I can remember is the first day that he hit me. I wasn't expecting it.
I came home from work, and he was in a foul mood. He was in the living room with a beer in hand. A scowl on his face. Sweat was rippling down my back, and I ignored the slight tremor in my hand.

"What happened, Love? You look like you had a bad day." I should have looked for warning signs. Like the snort he gave before he rose ominously out of the chair.
"What makes you think you have the right to ask me about my day?" It was the first time I heard that tone in his voice, but it wasn't the last.

"I was just wondering. Maybe you would feel better if you shared it with me." He took one step closer, and I flinched. I fucking flinched. That was the moment that he stole my power. Or I handed it over to him with a twitch. His eyes turned bright and the smirk that distorted his face haunts my memories still. He grabbed me by the arm and forced me to the kitchen table. He pressed my face into the wood, and the smell of Mr. Min made my eyes tear up.

"You want to make me feel better? The only way you can make me feel better is to be quiet, Bitch." His grip on the back of my neck is excruciating. I helplessly tried to push him back, but at that angle, I was pinned down. When I try to push myself up, I slip in the body sweat outline I leave behind on the table. My heart is racing, and I force the air down my throat. Every time I tried to open my mouth, he would force my head harder against the wood. It didn't take long before he hunched over me and exhaled in relief. The words he flung in my direction were the final blow that broke me.
"Remember, Wife, you are mine."

I sat at that table with stained thighs and cheeks and no reasonable explanation. This wasn't the man that I married. I carefully traced the bruises he left behind on my neck and arms and ached for a deeper understanding. What could have angered him so much that he had to take it out on me? Is there ever a good enough reason for him to do that to me? Maybe it was just this one time. It will never happen again. It was just this one day.

I often think about that naive woman while I trace the little marks my teeth left, praying to see some image of hope with a dotted outline. I still haven't fixed the tear in my skirt. My hands keep shaking when I try to thread the needle with the red color thread.

If only I could fix my heart with the same thread. I would weave a stronger outer wall that would be impenetrable by his snide comments and vicious hands. In one day, he changed into the demon that shreds my soul into lost pieces that yearn to escape on the wind.
I look down at the still expression on her tiny face. She is barely twenty weeks old. It took some time to find someone who was willing to take the risk for me. I look back at my savior as he comes closer and tries to prey her away from me. I didn't realize the shrill sound came from me until the other woman touched my arm.
"You need to let go now. It is time."

I look down at her again, and I know two definite truths at this moment. As my finger traced her head gently, I knew I did right by my daughter. I would never be able to keep him away from her. And this is a gentler way to go to the same destination. And secondly, he will regret the day I had to murder my one true love. The woman brings a piece of material and slowly wraps it around my daughter. She turns to me, nods once, and follows the other two out of the door. I am left alone in a room that smells like shame and regret with the knowledge that the last scrap of my being that held any value is going to be buried in an unmarked grave by strangers. As if I deserved such kindness for this one day.

South African **VERSES**

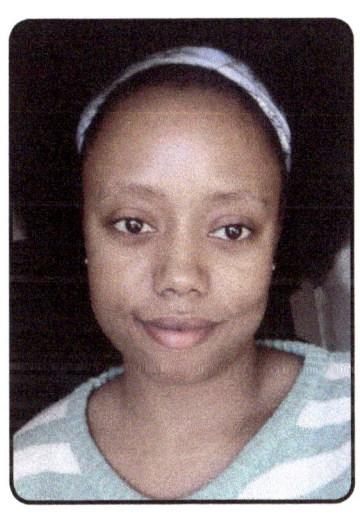

Instagram: @naledibiyela_

Sthuthukile Mkhize is a freelance writer and editor with a degree in English Studies. When she's not editing manuscripts or essays, she enjoys writing in her journal or working on her personal blog, "Star in The Tribe."

In addition to her writing, she volunteers as a Trauma Debriefer at her local police station, where she ensures that trauma victims receive the care and attention they need. Her biggest goal is to become a published author and release her poetry collection in the coming year.

In a Broken Home

In a broken home,
It's the quiet that gets you.
The peace seems to taunt
That fragile hope,
As we wait for the next blow to fall.
But we hope anyway.
With porcelain smiles, we try
And sway to hidden music,
Like puppets on a string.
Fearfully, we flicker, then shine,
Yearning for things to be different this time.
So we dust off the good china,
Crack open the special wine,
And raise a toast to a loving home.
And then...
No one remembers how it starts.
We all vacate our skin, evaporate into thin air,
To somewhere far and safe.
Mine is a lovely stretch of beach
In the Caribbean Sea.
Later, I will go for a swim...
And soon, I can't even hear the screams.

In a Broken Home

In a broken home, you can drown in a coffee cup,
Burn beneath a well-aimed glare,
Trip over a strand of hair.
The rules of the world don't apply there.
I was something different,
An anomaly that shouldn't have existed.
It was abominable, what happened in that home.
They say the carpet is still stained
From the remains.
Crayons immortalised on the wall,
A table still set for four.
We still lived there,
Drinking from empty glasses,
Toasting to time that never passes.
We go out once a week,
Dressed in our Sunday finery.
In a straight line, just as we rehearsed,
Have a glorious time,
And then we leave in a flurry,
Before the spell wears off
And someone notices the smell
Of rotten flesh and bone.
We ride off, we do,
In a pumpkin carriage, leaving behind a tattered shoe.
Then at last, we arrive at our humble abode
And seal the door closed.
- But no one is home.

"Bad Girl"

Our first catcalls came
From inside the house,
A million mothers and aunties
Digging inside my blouse, impatient
For the first seeds of womanhood to sprout.
Rough hands covered my mouth, lest
My baby teeth should fall out.
Somewhere between six and sixteen,
I turned into a wanton thing,
Guilty for having skin.

It was then, I understood
My body as a weapon, loaded to shoot,
And I its first victim.
It was a harmless tradition
That curled my arms inward,
Covered my legs, scared
Of existing.

It was a woman's gaze that trapped
My figure in a vase
And left flowers for the wake.
But she once had my face...

Tiktok: @mervinmf
Instagram: mervinmfrancis
Facebook: Mervin Mark Francis

Mervin M. Francis unveils his third poetic offering, Life, Dreams and Challenges, a reflective and insightful exploration of life's myriad hurdles and aspirations.

Beginning his literary journey with Book of Dreams, his debut collection, Francis established himself as a whimsical poet. His second volume, Dreams of Life, marked a significant evolution in his work, as he embraced themes of positivity and inspiration. With his latest book, however, Francis delves even deeper into the complexities of existence, reflecting on both the triumphs and trials that shape our dreams.

Residing on the North Coast of Durban, Mervin continues to write in his spare time, balancing his creative endeavours with a management role at Toyota South Africa. Through his poetry, he seeks the freedom to share his thoughts, emotions, and reflections with the world, allowing his words to resonate far beyond the page.

A Diamond in the Ruff
(A Tribute to Alta H Haffner)

In the midst of my dilemma, I stood all alone.
Assessing my journey, and how I have grown.
The path that I took unleashed a passion of note.
Yet the results of my work, showed no positive growth.

No matter how hard I tried, I took on some strain.
I tirelessly trudged on, through the disappointment and pain.
I had family and friends that stood proud by my side.
Encouraging me to persevere and take things in my stride.

My prayers were answered during my time of grief.
When an amazing soul was sent, to help me turn a new leaf.
A diamond in the ruff, with a heart bleeding nothing but joy.
She extended a supporting hand, so my creativeness I could deploy.

Alta H Haffner, together with the amazing Charles Haffner.
Wondered into my life, by the graces of the heavenly father.
Brimming with pride, I no longer stand alone as I go forth
In a short space of time, she has shown me what's my true worth.

A true inspiration, who puts in all her love and energy.
To catapult her authors to great heights, she will work tirelessly.
My love and respect, she has truly earned.
My dreams within me, she has undoubtedly reaffirmed.

A Positive Mind

She stormed away, leaving him behind.
Don't bother looking, there is nothing you will find.
My feelings for you have withered and died.
Words piercing his heart, deep inside.

Wasted years, a life gone up in smoke.
His heart shattered into pieces from how she spoke.
He watched on silently as she strode away.
Her painful words, forever with him shall stay.

Taking deep breaths, his puzzle finally done.
With the writing on the wall, reality was no fun.
He amazingly felt somewhat at ease.
In his mind a conviction, to live as he please.

It is time to let go of burdens from the past.
Think of the future, and don't put yourself last.
Changes are good if you start with a positive mind.
Unlock life's journey, great opportunities you will find.

Lessons Learnt

Mistakes were made and lessons learnt.
When playing with fire, be mindful not to get burnt.
Life isn't that simple, as reality will tell.
Step out of line and nothing goes well.

Lessons learnt, will give you guidance.
Giving your new life a whole lot of sustenance.
Allowing you the courage for a new direction.
So that from within, to improve your situation.

With open arms, embrace these moments.
Listen attentively, pay heed to their comments.
Be the change that you seek to find.
Share the thoughts embedded in your mind.

Sarita Mathur is a dedicated expert in visualisation and motivation, specialising in Abundance and Emotional Intelligence. A Reiki Master and Karuna Reiki Master Teacher, she has taught transformative courses such as The Caterpillar Has Become a Butterfly.

Her book, Once Again...Love, combines poetry and prose to explore the metaphysical aspects of life, bridging science and spirituality. Sarita's work has gained worldwide recognition, including being a semi-finalist in the Lentswe Poetry Project and having poems featured in Unbreaking the Rainbow, The Hudson View, and a Haitian-themed anthology.

A guest speaker at the Live Poets Society in Durban, South Africa, and featured on Eastern Mosaic TV, Sarita has also been profiled in Women Who Made a Difference. She coined the acronym M.O.N.E.Y. (My Own Natural Energy Yields) to represent abundance from within. Honoured with The Silver Quill Award and featured at the Delhi and Calcutta Literature Festivals, Sarita's book has been accepted into libraries in South Africa.

The Monkey

They've taken away my habitat,
That is what I say,
They've taken away my habitat,
And I can no longer stay...
In trees surrounding dwellings,
Houses built up high,
Or low on the ground.
I cannot run around,
Swinging from tree to tree,
Eating bananas and other fruit,
Without pellets being shot at me.

Yes, I can no longer be myself,
Without water being thrown at me.
Or the cry "monkey thief"
Being shouted at me.
They've taken away my habitat.

What would you do,
If this happened to you?
Would you defend yourself
And be proudly you,
Or just run away, never to return,
While your habitat
Was stolen from you?
Would you
Keep cutting down trees,
Spoiling the ecology,
Reducing biodiversity,
The habitat of the birds and bees?

They've taken away my habitat,
I want to know,
What you would do,
If this happened to you!

The Soul Story

The soul has a history,
Its own story,
Of lifetimes lived
And lessons learnt.

It has its own journey:
As it says,
'Oh, my family on earth,
Do not grieve for me,
I loved you and must move on
As I fulfil my own destiny.'

My time on earth is over,
But yours still carries on.
My physical presence may not be there,
Though my spirit lingers on.
Be strong and let good thoughts remain
Of the good times spent together.

I nurtured you from the time you were born,
And in spirit, we will be together:
Though my physical body has to
Move on.

Sinobom Vutha **is a talented writer and emerging artist based in Durban, originally from the Eastern Cape. Her journey in writing began in primary school, where she honed her skills through participation in reading and writing competitions, sparking a lifelong passion for literature. Primarily known for her poetry, Sinobom has used her craft to engage with social issues and foster meaningful connections.**

From 2019 to 2021, she extended her reach to radio, creating thought-provoking pieces on various topics. In her role at her job, she crafts captivating copies for social media and composes letters on behalf of the management, showcasing her creativity and expertise. Her belief in the power of art to drive social commentary has also influenced her visual artistry. As an emerging visual artist, Sinobom has showcased her work at the Kwande Festival and the Menzi Mchunu Gallery, where she also contributed a thrilling written piece for the theme "Our Democracy, Our Freedom, Our Voices."

Sinobom draws inspiration from everyday interactions, human emotions, and the beauty of nature, with her creative work reflecting a deep commitment to both personal expression and social consciousness.

Ubuntu

Recently, I began to believe that ubuntu was a thing of the past,
That it was "each to his own,"
And "It is what it is" echoed from every corner of the nation,
Man left to his own devices.
But no man is an island,
Maybe that's why so much is wrong with the world.

Maybe that's why, recently, I started to believe
That ubuntu was a thing of the past.
But that doesn't mean I don't still look for it,
And I find it in the woman who sees someone she takes a taxi with,
Still walking to the taxi rank, and asks the driver to stop for them.

I see it in the driver who knows all his passengers and their stops,
So even on days they are tired and fall asleep,
He makes sure they don't miss their stop.
I see it in the woman who has never seen me before,
But hands me a few extra notes when she sees I'm leaving a few items at the till.

I see it in the man who stops when he sees another harassing a defenseless woman..

I see it in the boy who shares his lunch with the one who sits in the corner,
I see it in the little girl, full of innocence,
Who believes in the kindness of strangers.
I see ubuntu in the smiles of strangers,
The greatest kindness in a world that views it as a weakness.

Recently, I started to believe that ubuntu was a thing of the past,
But maybe I am wrong,
And ubuntu still has a fighting chance.

Umbilo Taxi

As the sun gently rises behind the buildings to my right,
Approaching the taxi, I survey where I want to sit
Not fully taking note of the passengers,
I've committed them to memory.
I have sat beside each one at some point in time.

Taking my seat, I count the empty spaces left
And count the fare.
The driver navigates the road as I listen to Dylan Sinclair.

The skylight is playing a beautiful freeze
Of tall palm trees, blue grey skies, and streetlights.
This jungle is beautiful in these early hours.
To my left, I see people rushing about their business.
To my right, the sun is bouncing off the still surface of the waters,
Glistening like precious stones.
A mesmerizing scene I don't want to look away from,
Which passes by swiftly.

My eyes are back to the skylight, watching the signs blur by without blinking.
In a heartbeat, it seems I'm almost at my stop.

My breath catches, and I silently prepare to speak up.
The driver briefly sweeps his eye on the review mirror and signals that I speak up.

I do so and wait,
With bated breath,
For him to stop at the right place.
Hopefully, he won't continue,
Because I'd just let him keep driving.

I take my bags and slightly rise
As he approaches my stop,
So as to remind him, in a way.

I look to the sky,
And I'm delighted by the crisp air as I step off.

South African **VERSES**

TikTok and X: @bee.with.the.books

Bianca Nikita **is an avid reader whose love for books has led her to become a bookish influencer and reviewer for multiple publishing houses.**

From a young age, she was captivated by the adventures books provided, and this passion for reading and writing has stayed with her into adulthood.

Recently, Bianca has begun to explore and share her journey in the literary world, continuing to inspire others with her enthusiasm for books.

A Shattered Shell

A glistening shell, so far from reach,
Washed upon the shore, right at your feet.
Desired by many, given to one,
Only to end up tethered and worn.

A bright and glistening shell,
First in your hands, so gentle.
Carried home, to a place to belong,
But then hidden away, was something wrong?

Love that breaks and mends together,
Left a shell, so torn and weathered.
You took her iridescent pearl,
The one she gave because you were her world.

Another shell she sees in your hand,
As she looks, hidden beneath the sand.
This other shell you've shown so proud,
Loved so publicly, so openly, so loud.

A shattered shell, now buried away,
With bruises, cracks, and no desire to stay.
An emptiness now lies within,
Her missing pieces now a part of your skin.

South African **VERSES**

www.mashezee.co.za

MaShezee is a versatile artist whose creative journey bridges the worlds of music and poetry. With a growing presence on digital music platforms, MaShezee made her mark as a musician, blending sound and emotion to tell compelling stories.

While music remains her primary passion, poetry serves as another expressive outlet—one she continues to nurture and refine.

Her poetic works reflect a deep connection to rhythm and wordplay, offering audiences an intimate glimpse into her creative spirit. As she evolves in both crafts, MaShezee remains dedicated to pushing artistic boundaries and sharing her voice with the world.

Power of Words

There is power in words,
So the positive is preferred.
Speak the unheard,
Not the negative that has occurred.

Break the cycle before further damage is incurred.
Words can be a plus or minus,
Can cheer you up or put you down,
Make you smile or frown.
Words can bring the wrong attraction,
Or push away the right association.

What do you prefer?
Your present state or creating your future estate?
Call those things into existence,
Even though they do not exist yet.
There will be resistance,
But keep speaking and be persistent.

There is power in words,
Have you not heard?
Though most times people will think you're nuts,
At least you have the guts,
To dare to dream - and plus,
You have nothing to lose, so don't fuss.

Do not speak the negative,
The atmosphere is very sensitive.
It will produce what you say,
And not the alternative.

The more you say, the more your situation is repetitive,
Because your life is a representative of what you say,
So it becomes imperative
To speak the positive.

Speak life and not strife,
Speak favour and do not waver,
Speak prosperity and not adversity,
Speak success and do not digress,
Speak victory and not misery,
Speak blessing and stop stressing.

There is power in words,
So the positive is preferred.
Speak the unheard,
Not the negative that has occurred.
Break the cycle before further damage is incurred!

Live That Dream

Live that dream.
Live it now.
Live it loud.
Live it proud.

Excuse the crown.
Never mind their do's and don'ts,
That lavish you with lies of limitation.
Hmm, you're good, but not good enough.
The industry is just too tough.
But I say to you,
Stretch forth, break forth.
Impossible is the new possible!

Live that dream.
Live it now.
Live it loud.
Live it proud.

Don't let heartbreak and disappointments leave you crying,
And stop you from trying.
Life can be short or long.
You choose which end you will belong to.
Dreams and great teams lie in the bed of the grave.
Big ideas, big thoughts, but lacked a heart that's brave.
Some thought, but never fought.
While others fought, no matter what life brought.

Some destinies seemed short,
But purpose-driven,
Better than some who are still living.
It's not in how you start,
It's in the finish line.
How will you end up, or will you end down?
Just a statistic in some town,
Or will you demand your crown?

Live that dream.
Live it now.
Live it loud.
Live it proud.

While you have a heartbeat,
You have a drumbeat,
To the rhythm leading to your destiny's seat.
On your marks was your birth.
Get set was your growth.
Go is when a seed of thought is planted, and a dream is born.
A desire is set in your heart like fire.
So, lift up your shield and sword.
Defend your dream to its very last word.

Live that dream.
Live it now.
Live it loud.
Live it proud.

Set your heart as a soldier.
Do not let doubt filter the dream that you love.
Find the how and let it start,
Becoming reality, even if in parts.
Your dream has purpose,
Not just for you, but also for those who will live after you.
Martin Luther had a dream,
And now we can dream because of his dream,
And pursue the dream the way he fought for his dream.
We may not know the final hour,
But that should not, and cannot, take away the power of your dream.
So, I boldly say,

Live that dream.
Live it now.
Live it loud.
Live it proud.

https://www.tiktok.com/@zubairbobat

Zubair Bobat, also known as Bazm-E-Yaaraan, is a talented Bollywood singer and vocalist available for a variety of events, including weddings, mehndi's, parties, fairs, and shows.

He has earned significant recognition for his musical achievements, including being the 1st runner-up of Rising Stars...It's Your Voice 2023, winning KZN Bollywood Idol Season 1 2023, and being awarded the Artes Award 2024. Additionally, Zubair has been named the Singing Sensation Brand Ambassador KZN 2024, solidifying his reputation as a rising star in the industry.

SS Tilawa

A ship we will always remember,
SS Tilawa was it's name.
Transporting bullion,cargo and passengers
was it's humble game.

Built big and strong in 1924'
it took on service for many years long.
Sailed through waters straight and true,
it's direction never wrong.

It took on seas
both calm and rough,
succeeding at it's tasks,
no matter how tough.

In it's image it was simple,
some might say flauntless
but its heart as pure
as we knew it to be dauntless

It carried it's goods and people
from there to here,
moving all who were
to us very dear.

My great grandfather was a passenger
on the list getting all set for the trip.
he gave his hugs and kisses
and stepped over the ship's entrance lip.

He looked back at his friends and family,
said his goodbyes as he wave,
to the people who in their heart's,
a love he engraved.

He had sadness of leaving his homeland
but a joy as in Africa his family await,
with many others starting a new life in
a new world trying to change their fate.

What fate you may ask, they were
under the rule of the British.
Their freedoms were taken
and to stay they did not wish.

A few were headed back from their visit,
anxious to get home.
The boat was overcrowded
like bees on a honeycomb.

The ship set off and further
away it moved from the docks.
Everyone settled in and set
the time of arrival on their clocks.

Chuffing along with a small steam engine,
it ate away slowly at the miles,
at 12 knots, its maximum speed,
facing the sea's tribulations and trials.

It was not just any normal journey,
but one that was travelled in fear.
The ship ploughed on as fast as it could,
through the waters like a spear,

Already 5 days had past,
all was good and well.
Many more days still to go,
a story only time could tell.

They prayed for a safe journey
as they travelled during the second world war,
a huge battle between nations that
shook the world to its core.

Candles burned were only allowed bellow decks,
on the way to their desired landmarks.
Sails painted black,all were to be calm and quiet,
while the upper levels should be completely dark.
A good reason at the time to
prevent them from becoming a mark.
So they stayed as invisible as possible,
for an attack not to spark

The cargo stowed away tight.
passengers turned in for the night.
gunners at posts through dark,no light
and the captain with only the destination in sight.

But...

It was a cold night,
a night with a bright moonlight
and still far from morning twilight,
SS Tilawa was about to face it's toughest fight.

It was 23rd November 1942,
over 700 passengers and over 200 crew,
for they did not know in the
waters on route what brew.

It was in the early morning
at 1:30, they heard a bang.
A torpedo which was sent
and in their ears a fear rang.

They were not alone for in the depths
lurked a Japanese submarine.
They could not attack or defend
as the enemy could not be seen.

There was but just one option left
and that was to get off the ship.
In a hurry they started to disembark
while the vessel's head into the water started to dip.

Safety boats were set in place,
over the edge it was lifted.
Unhooked after being filled,falling free,
slowly away it drifted.

Rushing for safety in fear,
indeed a dramatic event.
facing an opponent
who had malicious intent.

It could have been to take it's cargo
or just a military threat.
We still understand not why
or what was their mindset.

The radio officer stayed back to give the travellers a chance
to get off during this current hess
and he rushed to his cabin in panic
sending an SOS to notify of their distress.

Passengers got onto lifeboats,the ship stood strong
as they latched onto life by a single thread of rope.
To come back if the ship still stood
but a second torpedo removed all that hope.

The second sunk it a very few moments later
ending the SS Tilawa's life,
along with many still aboard
whose cries were as sharp as a knife

Caught in a dangerous situation,
all passengers in disarray
for the loss of lives,they,the opponent
will never be able to repay.

Some got to lifeboats while other
attacked by barracudas went below
and with the weight of some lifeboats,
into it water started to flow.

many tried getting onto something
that floated using it as a raft.
Though in a frenzy,was the best
they could have choreographed.

Sharks arrived,they circled around,
attracted by the blood.
In their hearts and minds an uncertainty
of life started to flood.

The wind blew cold,huge waves they face,
with a hope to be rescued with tearful eyes,
as they floated on a vast ocean,
no land in sight,fearing their worst demise

Drenched and shivering,in agony and shock,
they bowed their heads and sincerely prayed,
for a rescue vessel to turn their way and come to view
while their floats rapidly bounced and swayed.

Arguments arouse between crew
as to which direction to follow.
With no sight and no knowledge,
their understanding was hollow.

But still they held on strong.
biscuits and water were rationed.
For 2 day and 3 nights afloat,
without a good meal fashioned.

A few days after,not long
after the sun has risen
A plane was approaching them and signalling,
later a ship popped up on the horizon.

They were finally picked up by the
SS Birmingham who did their rescue rounds,
before taking the survivors of
SS Tilawa to much safer grounds.

Had the rescue been a few hours delayed,
they would have been swept away by a storm,
but was met by a miracle from God,
who sent a battleship crewed by men in uniform.

With pain in their hearts of a
fate they faced at great cost,
of people they held dear like
friends and families that was lost.

Many lost their lives and but just a few
who were fortunate lived to tell the tale.
The horrors seen,the screams heard,
chaos and panic which rendered them pale.

Many were lost to those even not aboard the Tilawa,
as the Birmingham drew close to port and arrived,
and more hearts were broken as eyes searched frantically
through only a handful who survived.

The ship may sail no more,but
remembered for all it's might and glory.
My great grandfather survived the ordeal
along with a few others to tell it's story

If not in body,those that have not reached,
still leave in us a big hole.
They will be remembered,kept in the heart
for they still have a living soul.

The SS Tilawa would now
never reach it's destined port.
It helped many people over the years
and fought all that it could have fought.

Now to the marine life being a home,
it rests at the bottom on the sea bed.
The next phase of it's journey,
we should not consider it dead

The cuts and bruises, burns and loss
still to this day remained
and what transpired at the time
still cannot be explained.
The answers to the questions we ask
hope to be soon obtained
of a story that had and will
always continue to be maintained.

We hold an anniversary of this incident
even till now, the year 2024.
taking up the tradition of remembering it,
just like many have done before.

Many here just like myself are from lineage,
descendants only a few generations later.
who are related to someone
that was aboard the freighter.

But...

For those who were onboard and those who awaited it's arrival,
life would not continue to be the same.
For this is the tragic story of a ship, "THE INDIAN TITANIC",
and SS Tilawa was it's name.

South African **VERSES**

Timia Chetty is an 11-year-old South African writer. Inspired by the rich culture and history of her country, she writes stories that explore identity, humanity, and the complexities of life.

Timia's work highlights the beauty and resilience of South Africa, reflecting her deep connection to her heritage.

The Forgotten Guitar

In a neglected township, a young boy named Sipho stumbled upon something that instantly captivated his attention. It appeared to be a guitar in the trash, miraculously still in good condition. The young boy wondered how something so well-preserved ended up discarded in the rubbish. He retrieved the guitar and took it back to his humble home.

Sipho then began experimenting with the instrument, playing a soulful melody. He envisioned his father, a musician who had passed on, and imagined him playing alongside him, guiding him with each note. Sipho shared his passion with the people of his village, who were in awe of this young boy's talent and how he seemed to embody his father's spirit.

Whenever he played, Sipho would drift into the realm of his father's tales from the days of Apartheid, when music served as a form of defiance. He imagined his father's fingers moving in rhythm over the frets, creating a mesmerizing harmony that inspired hope in all who heard it. Through music, Sipho felt connected to his father, keeping his legacy and memories alive.

As he continued playing, the sounds of the instrument seemed to carry his father's spirit into the night sky, creating a heartwarming moment for Sipho.

https://wilhelmbooks.co.za

Wilhelm was born in Windhoek, where the vast desert winds whisper stories of resilience. His early years were steeped in the open skies and rugged landscapes of Namibia.

However, it was the old Western Transvaal, where he grew up and studied, that truly shaped the man he would become. There, beneath the endless sun, life was a blend of tradition and quiet determination—qualities that would later echo in his writing.

He is the author of A Cult's Tentacles and From Hippie to Preacher available worldwide.

Sipo and the Bicycle Rim

Every day, the whole settlement knew where Sipo was. They could hear the clinking sound of his bicycle rim long before they saw him, and then, there he'd be—running fast, controlling the rim with a stick like it was the most prized possession in the world.

As soon as the school bell rang, Sipo would dash home, excited to begin his daily adventure. After quickly changing out of his school clothes, he'd grab the rim that hung on the big mango tree in his yard. The rim, old and a little bent, was his treasure. He didn't have a bicycle, but with his rim and stick, he didn't need one. In Sipo's eyes, that rim was his speedy Kawasaki motorbike.

Down the dusty street he'd go, stick in hand, carefully balancing the rim, running as fast as he could. The people in the settlement always knew when Sipo was coming. Some would whistle, amused by his joyful running, while others would move out of the way, balancing baskets or pots on their heads, laughing as they watched him pass by.

Even the taxi drivers would slow down, smiling as Sipo dashed along. They knew how much fun he was having. But sometimes, Sipo's excitement got the better of him, and he'd lose control of the rim.

One afternoon, as he was zooming around a corner, the rim slipped away from him. It started rolling faster than Sipo could catch it, heading straight for Gogo's fat cake stall.

"NOOOO!" Sipo yelled, chasing after it. But it was too late.

The rim crashed into Gogo's small table, sending the fat cakes flying out of the bowl. They bounced and rolled all over the ground. Gogo, the kind old woman who always sold the fluffiest, sweetest fat cakes in the settlement, just shook her head.

"Sipo!" she scolded, though she couldn't help but smile. "You must be more careful! You might hurt somebody one day."

Sipo stopped, breathless and full of guilt. He ran to help pick up the fat cakes, dusting off the ones that had rolled away.

"I'm sorry, Gogo," he said, his face turning red. Gogo chuckled softly, patting his head. "It's okay, child. Just be careful, hmm?"
Sipo nodded, grateful that Gogo wasn't angry. She knew him well. After all, every day, without fail, she'd see him racing around with that bicycle rim of his.

Once everything was back in place, Sipo picked up his rim, gave Gogo a sheepish smile, and set off again—this time a little more slowly. But in his mind, he was still on his Kawasaki, zooming through the settlement, the wind in his hair, the sound of laughter and cheers all around him.

For Sipo, nothing in the world was as wonderful as that old, wobbly rim. And no matter how many times it got away from him.

One afternoon, while the clouds looked like fluffy candy floss, Sipo walked over to his trusty old bicycle rim. He had it hanging on the mango tree in the yard, and he always kept the stick he used to steer the rim safely tucked under his bed. With excitement bubbling inside, Sipo grabbed the rim in one hand and his stick in the other.

He held the rim steady, lifted his leg, and gave it a strong kick, pretending it was his Kawasaki motorcycle. "Brrrrrrr!" he buzzed with his lips, making a loud motorbike sound as he pushed the rim forward with the stick.

Off he went, racing down the main road of the settlement, the wind rushing through his hair. But just as he was reaching top speed, disaster struck! Sipo's foot hit a half-buried brick in the road. Down he tumbled, rolling in the dust as the rim sped off without him.

Sipo sat there, shocked and in pain, holding his bruised toe, but the real chaos was just beginning.

The rim, free from Sipo's guiding hand, was out of control! It rolled faster and faster, straight towards a flock of chickens. Feathers flew in all directions as the chickens squawked and scattered, darting out of the way.

People heard the clattering metal and turned to look, but there was no sign of Sipo—just the wild, runaway rim zooming by.

A dog, lazily resting in the warm sand by the roadside, suddenly jumped up with a yelp as the rim nearly ran over him. Children nearby were laughing and shouting as they chased after the runaway rim, trying to catch it.

Then, with a mighty clang, the rim hit a brick and bounced high into the air.

It soared through the sky and landed right on top of a taxi! The driver slammed on the brakes, and everyone inside screamed in surprise.

The driver leaped out of the taxi, but all he could see was the rim speeding off again, down the road, causing even more chaos.

Taxis swerved left and right to avoid hitting the flying rim. People were jumping out of the way, and the noise of metal screeching against the gravel made everyone's ears ring. The whole settlement was buzzing with excitement and confusion.

Even the traffic cop, who had been chatting with a taxi driver, was caught off guard. When the rim zoomed past him, he switched on his siren and gave chase, thinking it was some kind of mischief. The whole settlement watched in disbelief as the cop chased after... a bicycle rim!

Meanwhile, back where Sipo had fallen, he sat by the roadside, tears streaming down his dust-covered cheeks as he nursed his busted big toe. His fun day had turned into a disaster. After catching his breath and wiping away his tears, Sipo hopped home on one leg.

The next day, to Sipo's surprise, there was a picture in the local newspaper. The headline read: **"Bicycle Rim Causes Havoc in Settlement!"**

And there, in the photo, was the traffic cop chasing the runaway rim. Sipo couldn't help but smile. Even though his toe still hurt, he knew this was one story he would laugh about for a long, long time.

www.ingramcontent.com/pod-product-compliance
Lightning Source LLC
Chambersburg PA
CBHW040748020526
44118CB00041B/2795